THE SCREEN
COMPLETE, ALL-IN-ONE, STEP-BY-STEP, CONCISE, EASY-TO-FOLLOW, EASY-TO-USE, COMPREHENSIVE
STORY PLANNING GUIDE

(OR: HOW TO BEGIN WORKING ON AN IDEA YOU DON'T HAVE.)

Developed by

STEVEN R. GOTTRY
Perspiring Screenwriter

THE SCREENWRITER'S STORY PLANNING GUIDE
Copyright © 1999 by Steven R. Gottry
ISBN: 0-9667483-0-1

My fun-filled World Wide Web site is at: http://www.6FU.com • e-mail: steve@6FU.com

Cover design and illustration by Matt Newton, who spent a lot of time on it and had to put up with a picky author who kept saying, "Could you change this? Could you change that? Could you make this a little redder? Could you make my name a little bigger?"

• Discounts are available on bulk copies used for educational purposes.
Please contact the publisher for more information.

PRIORITY MULTIMEDIA GROUP, INC.®
Post Office Box 41540
Mesa, AZ 85274-1540
Phone: (602) 831-5557
Fax: (601) 831-7373
www.prioritymm.com

Printed in the United States of America • 99 00 01 02 03 04 • 10 9 8 7 6 5 4 3 2 1

"I want to thank the Academy..."

No, actually, that's a bit premature.

But there are some wonderful people I'd like to thank...

Karla, for having the courage to stay married to a writer...

Kalla, for understanding why I had to miss the Girl Scout Father/Daughter Dance...

Jon and Michelle for making me proud...

Ken and Susan Wales for support that really makes a difference...

Richard Baltzell for advice that is actually worthwhile...

Dave Anderson, Jeff Holder, John Schmidt and Dave Ross for opportunities...

Pam Benoit—always there, always cares, always very dramatic...

Ken Blanchard for the creative energy he inspires...

Dave Durenberger for faithful encouragement...

Father Duane Pederson for still being my friend after all these years...

Eric Walljasper for hanging in there through all the takeoffs and landings...

Don Stolz, "Mr. Old Log Theater," for pushing me to be my best...

Dave Gjerness, Terry Esau, and James Gottry for reading all my scripts...

Becky Owen for catching the mistakes and making the world a better place...

Final Draft, Inc. for wonderfully intuitive software and responsive customer care...

My friends—for accepting an "artisan temperament" in their midst...

Scott Blanchard for explaining what that actually means...

and, of course,

John and Bruce for their help in closing my ad agency so I could do what I really love.

How to use this book:

1) Fill a suitable glass with your favorite beverage.

2) Take the beverage, this book, and a pen/pencil/crayon to your favorite quiet working spot. Barbados would be nice.

3) Begin at page one and fill in the information (or check the boxes as desired) until you see a "story pattern" develop. Hint: You may do this in as many combinations as you want. Don't be afraid to make mistakes. Don't be afraid to cross things out and start over. Don't be afraid of anything.

4) When you have a story that makes sense, fill in the "Character" section.

5) After you've finished this book, you're ready to begin working on your 3" X 5" cards, your notebook, your typewriter, or your computer. Yes, they still make typewriters. I think.

6) When you have completed your screenplay, sell it for lots of money.

It's as easy as that! To your success!

This Screenplay is called:

" _____ "

- ☐ *"Untitled Screenplay"*
- ☐ *I'll give it a name later.*

It's about a(n):

- ☐ *Old Man*
- ☐ *Old Woman*
- ☐ *Man*
- ☐ *Woman*
- ☐ *Teenage Boy*
- ☐ *Teenage Girl*
- ☐ *Young Boy*
- ☐ *Young Girl*
- ☐ *Infant*
- ☐ *Animal:* _____
- ☐ *Alien from:* _____
- ☐ *Other:* _____

This [Character] is:

- ☐ *Married*
- ☐ *Single*
- ☐ *Widowed*
- ☐ *Divorced*
- ☐ *Gay/Lesbian*
- ☐ *In Prison*

This [Character] lives in/on:

- ☐ *Land:*
    - ☐ *City*
    - ☐ *Small Town*
    - ☐ *Country/Wilderness*

in [Nation]: _____

- ☐ *Sea:*
    - ☐ *Ship*
    - ☐ *Island*
    - ☐ *Underwater Kingdom*

[continued]

- ☐ *Air:*
    - ☐ *Aircraft*
    - ☐ *Balloon/Blimp*
    - ☐ *Celestial Kingdom*
- ☐ *Space:*
    - ☐ *Outer*
    - ☐ *Inner*
    - ☐ *Extra-Terrestrial*

This [Character] lives in the year: _____

The current status of the [Character]:
- ☐ *Free*
- ☐ *Slave/Prisoner*
- ☐ *Mental Bondage*
- ☐ *Physical Bondage*
- ☐ *As Looney-Tunes as they come*

What this [Character] really desires is:

- ☐ *Fame*
- ☐ *Fortune/Great Wealth*
- ☐ *Power*
- ☐ *Good Looks*
- ☐ *Sex/More Sex*
- ☐ *Prestige*
- ☐ *A Relationship*
- ☐ *Drugs*
- ☐ *Revenge*
- ☐ *To Kill Someone*
- ☐ *Political Office*
- ☐ *A BMW*
- ☐ *Freedom*
- ☐ *Peace of Mind/Heart/Spirit*
- ☐ *A Really Good Massage*
- ☐ *An Agent Who Actually "Works At It"*
- ☐ *Other:* _____

UNFORTUNATELY, this [Character] has an [Opponent/Nemesis/Adversary], who is the [Character's]:

☐ *Spouse*

☐ *Lover*

☐ *Boss*

☐ *Co-worker*

☐ *Cell Mate*

☐ *Ex-spouse/Ex-lover*

☐ *Parent/Step-parent*

☐ *Child/Stepchild*

☐ *Teacher/Advisor/Mentor*

☐ *Union Boss*

☐ *Invisible/Imaginary Enemy*

☐ *Priest/Minister/Rabbi*

☐ *Very Own Personal Government Agent*

☐ *Other:* _____

FORTUNATELY, this [Character] has an [Ally/ Friend/Companion], who is the [Character's]:

- ☐ *Spouse*
- ☐ *Lover*
- ☐ *Boss*
- ☐ *Co-worker*
- ☐ *Cell Mate*
- ☐ *Ex-spouse/Ex-lover*
- ☐ *Parent/Step-parent*
- ☐ *Child/Stepchild*
- ☐ *Teacher/Advisor/Mentor*
- ☐ *Union Boss*
- ☐ *Invisible/Imaginary Friend*
- ☐ *Priest/Minister/Rabbi*
- ☐ *Very Own Personal Government Agent*
- ☐ *Other:* _____

UNFORTUNATELY, the [Opponent/Nemesis/ Adversary], has an [Ally/Friend/Companion] who is the [Opponent/Nemesis/ Adversary's]:

- ☐ *Spouse*
- ☐ *Lover*
- ☐ *Boss*
- ☐ *Co-worker*
- ☐ *Cell Mate*
- ☐ *Ex-spouse/Ex-lover*
- ☐ *Parent/Step-parent*
- ☐ *Child/Stepchild*
- ☐ *Teacher/Advisor/Mentor*
- ☐ *Union Boss*
- ☐ *Invisible/Imaginary Friend*
- ☐ *Probation Officer*
- ☐ *Very Own Personal Government Agent*
- ☐ *Other:* _____

To complicate matters further, these characters may not be what they appear to be at first glance. IT TURNS OUT THAT:

- ☐ *The Opponent remains the Opponent*
- ☐ *The Opponent abandons the "Dark Side of the Force" to become an Ally*

- ☐ *The Ally remains loyal to the end*
- ☐ *The Ally is a rat-fink who turns to the "Dark Side of the Force"* "The Dark Side of the Force" may be a registered trademark of Lucasfilm Ltd. and/or Twentieth Century Fox.

- ☐ *The Opponent's Ally sticks with the Opponent to the bitter end.*
- ☐ *The Opponent's Ally abandons the Opponent in favor of the [Character]*

- ☐ *The [Character] becomes a jerk*
- ☐ *The [Character] is a complete fraud*

What's worse—(wouldn't ya' just know it!) —there's a SUBPLOT or two.

☐ *The [Character's] Ally wants:*

_____

☐ *The Opponent's Ally wants:*

_____

☐ *Some new Character out-of-the-blue shows up and wants:*

_____

☐ *Someone gets ill or up-and-dies, specifically:* _____

☐ *A Natural Disaster, specifically:*

_____

comes along and messes it all up.

☐ *Someone "finds God" or runs off to join the circus.*

☐ *Other:* _____

Remember, most films are about "change," often referred to as "growth."

The characters in this story who will grow (improve, get "better") are: _____

_____

_____

_____

The characters in this story who will pretty much stay the same are: _____

_____

_____

_____

The characters in this story who will actually regress (get "worse") are: _____

_____

_____

_____

Now let's think more in depth about the characters, and how they fit into the overall scheme of things.

- *HOW will some characters grow?*

- *WHY will some characters remain the same?*

- *HOW will some characters get "worse?"*

- *WHICH characters will simply just die or disappear?*

Oh, yeah...one more...
- *Why should the audience give a rip?*

The character _____ will GROW
(improve, get "better") because: _____

_____

_____

The character _____ will GROW
(improve, get "better") because: _____

_____

_____

The character _____ will GROW
(improve, get "better") because: _____

_____

_____

The character _____ will GROW
(improve, get "better") because: _____

_____

_____

The character _____ *will pretty much STAY THE SAME because:* _____

_____

_____

The character _____ *will pretty much STAY THE SAME because:* _____

_____

_____

The character _____ *will pretty much STAY THE SAME because:* _____

_____

_____

The character _____ *will pretty much STAY THE SAME because:* _____

_____

_____

The character _____ will
actually regress (get "worse") because:

_____

_____

The character _____ will
actually regress (get "worse") because:

_____

_____

The character _____ will
actually regress (get "worse") because:

_____

_____

The character _____ will
actually regress (get "worse") because:

_____

_____

The audience should give a rip about
_____ *because:*

_____

The audience should give a rip about
_____ *because:*

_____

The audience should give a rip about
_____ *because:*

_____

The audience should give a rip about
_____ *because:*

_____

The audience should give a rip about
_____ *because:*

_____

The audience should give a rip about
_____ *because:*

_____

Now that you have a <u>general</u> idea of where you're headed, this might be a good time to choose a <u>genre</u> for your story, so that you know whether to write funny scenes, serious scenes, or scenes with lots of big explosions. Here's a basic list:

☐ *Comedy*   ☐ *Drama*   ☐ *Action*
☐ *Adventure*   ☐ *Historical*   ☐ *Ancient/Biblical History*
☐ *Western*   ☐ *Musical*   ☐ *Musical Comedy*
☐ *Horror*   ☐ *Romance*   ☐ *Crime/Gangster*
☐ *Thriller*   ☐ *Courtroom*   ☐ *Natural Disaster*
☐ *Wartime*   ☐ *Animated*   ☐ *Man-made Disaster*
☐ *"Kiddie"*   ☐ *Sci-Fi*   ☐ *"Rite of Passage"*
☐ *Women's Theme*   ☐ *Gay Theme*   ☐ *Actual Current Event*
☐ *Soft Porn*   ☐ *Pornographic*   ☐ *"Episodic" (Short Stories)*
☐ *"Travelogue"*   ☐ *"Roadie"*   ☐ *Foreign-Themed*
☐ *Troubled Past*   ☐ *Psychotic*   ☐ *Animal Adventure*

Fortunately, you can "mix 'n' match!"

☐ *Action/Adventure/Romance*   ☐ *Science Fiction/Musical*
☐ *Animated/Horror*   ☐ *Wartime/Episodic*
☐ *Romance/"Roadie"*   ☐ *Western/Gay Theme*
☐ *Historical/Troubled Past*   ☐ *Foreign-Theme/Disaster ("Ishtar")*
☐ *Animals Used in Science*   ☐ *Psychotic/Courtroom*
☐ *Crime/Gangster/Comedy*   ☐ *"Roadie"/Animal Adventure*

A few words of caution are in order. There are some themes to be avoided:

- *Hollywood – as in "The Life Story of [Your Name Here], the Screenwriter."*
- *Jewish Girls Who Pretend to be Boys.*
- *Zoo Animals that Eat Children.*
- *Children Who Eat Their Pets.*
- *Chia Pets.*
- *Bill Clinton: The Military Years.*
- *Battery Recharging for Seniors.*
- *Nuns Who Sleep Around.*
- *The Nine Lives of Elvis Presley.*
- *"Take My Wife. Please."*
- *Normal Mothers of Normal Children.*
- *The Dawn of Electricity.*
- *Happy, Well-Adjusted Postal Workers.*
- *Pat Boone.*

(Well, there might be SOME stories there.)

On the other hand, there are some themes that have been overlooked without just cause:

- *Honest People Who Always Win.*
- *Really Decent Lawyers.*
- *Genuinely Interesting Accountants.*
- *TV Evangelists Who Aren't Crooks.*
- *Rich Farmers from Kansas.*
- *People Who Don't Cheat on Taxes.*
- *The Electric Car.*
- *Salsa – the Hot, the Bad, and the Ugly.*
- *"We Indians Were Here First."*
- *Vegas – The Big Winners.*
- *Mercedes-Benz—"More than a Car."*
- *The French Really Aren't So Nasty.*
- *Cruising Vacations (Hey, Kathie Lee can't possibly go on 'em all.)*
- *The O.J. Trial. (Ooops! Where have I been for the last few years?)*

Ya gotta know one thing:

Most movies are structured in three "acts." And most movie scripts run 100 to 120 pages in length. And "act two" is usually the longest of the three. So what does this all mean?

THE BASICS:

• INTRO: Before or during the TITLES, you hafta come up with a "hook" that gets me involved with your story – and your hero. Up to 5 pages or so.

• ACT ONE: You want me to like (or really, really hate) your hero. You've got 5 to 15 pages to do that.

• Your hero's gotta get in some trouble (15 to 30 pages), and then I have to be worried about your hero (or want the hero dead – the "anti-hero").

• Then something BIG has gotta happen.

This is the "first major turning point" (or "plot point," to quote Syd Field) (see recommended books later) that gets the audience involved in the rest of the story. Usually this "plot point" is represented by the action of a clearly defined enemy/nemesis/adversary/lover, who has different objectives than your hero.

- ACT TWO: Nothing but trouble for the hero. Conflict, doubt, bad vibes, loaded guns, whatever. First the hero seems to win, then the adversary, then the hero. Ooops! Then the adversary, because of "plot point two" at the end of Act Two. We didn't expect this, but there it is, bigger than life. Is the movie over? Do we all go home now?

- NOPE. (Even though you've chewed up pages 30 to pages 85 or 90 of this script to tell this story.)

- **_Because_ ACT THREE, in all it's glory, is still to come! Someone's gotta win. Someone's gotta lose.** Of course, in some movies, everyone wins. In others, everyone loses. It's a crazy business.

- **If you've always wanted to write a chase scene, this is where it usually goes. Ditto reconciliation. Ditto death, imprisonment, honorable discharge, the birth of a child, or a lottery win. Or, maybe "guess who" comes to dinner and is finally loved and accepted.** Wouldn't you know it! Recently, some films have a rip-roaring chase scene right at the beginning: the "Chase-Hook." It may be a trend.

- **This is your chance to make 'em cry, make 'em laugh, make 'em cheer, make 'em spit up – or make 'em go home and bad-mouth your movie. Better do it right.**

- **It's all so terribly simple, isn't it?**

- **The ROLLUP. This is the part where the credits all crawl up the screen. And the theater employees come in and clean up the mess. And everyone leaves – except for you,** because your name is gonna be on that screen any second now. (Hope they don't expect you to help clean up.)

All that's left now are the reviews. And, of course, the Academy Award nominations.

Just remember:

0 - 5 pages:	The "hook."
5 - 30:	"Getting to know you."
Page 30:	Major "plot point."
30 - 90:	Complications, troubles, conflict, apparent defeat.
Page 90:	Major "plot point."
90 - 115:	Climax, resolution.
115+:	"Cooling down" period.*

* Can't just send the folks out of the theater right after the climax. They need to settle down for a couple of minutes. Page counts are approximate.

That's the three-act formula. For TV "Movies-of-the-week" (MOW), figure on seven or eight acts with a major plot point before each commercial break (to make sure the audience sticks with you). But that's another story.

Although much of this will come to you as you begin to write, it is often helpful to plan and describe the various locations you will use in your script – interiors, exteriors, and those "backgrounds" that pass by.

•Interiors:

_____

_____

_____

_____

_____

•Exteriors:

_____

_____

_____

_____

_____

•"Moving backgrounds":

_____

_____

_____

_____

This next assignment is a biggie.

In order to know what your characters want – and why – and in order to write believable dialogue, it's vital that you know your characters intimately.

The ten pages that follow are "biography" outlines for up to ten major characters who will populate your story.

After you've created "pasts" for them and have filled in all the details of their lives today, spend time studying them so that, as you write, you will know them as if they were real people.

In fact, feel free to use some characteristics of actual people you know! *Your seventh grade Phys Ed teacher could be fun. (Think about it!)*

CHARACTER BIO #1:

Full Name _____ Nickname _____

Born in: _____

Resides at/in: _____

Sex _____ Age _____ Race _____ Religion _____

Marital Status _____ Spouse's Name _____

Previous Marriages _____ Name(s) _____

Child One: _____ Sex: _____ Age: _____

Child Two: _____ Sex: _____ Age: _____

Additional Children: _____

Mother's Name _____

☐ Living, ☐ Dead, ☐ Quite sick, ☐ Institutionalized, ☐ Irrelevant

Father's Name _____

☐ Living, ☐ Dead, ☐ Quite sick, ☐ Institutionalized, ☐ Irrelevant

Older Sibling's Name(s) _____

☐ Living, ☐ Dead, ☐ Quite sick, ☐ Institutionalized, ☐ Irrelevant

Younger Sibling's Name(s) _____

☐ Living, ☐ Dead, ☐ Quite sick, ☐ Institutionalized, ☐ Irrelevant

Other Significant Person's Name _____

☐ Living, ☐ Dead, ☐ Quite sick, ☐ Institutionalized, ☐ Irrelevant

Character's General Health: _____

College: _____ Military Service: _____

Early Jobs: _____

Current Job: _____

Desired Job: _____

Hobbies/Interests: _____

Likes/Dislikes: _____

Major Strengths: _____

Major Weaknesses: _____

FATAL FLAW: _____

CHARACTER BIO #2

Full Name _____ Nickname _____

Born in: _____

Resides at/in: _____

Sex _____ Age _____ Race _____ Religion _____

Marital Status _____ Spouse's Name _____

Previous Marriages _____ Name(s) _____

Child One: _____ Sex: _____ Age: _____

Child Two: _____ Sex: _____ Age: _____

Additional Children: _____

Mother's Name _____

☐ Living, ☐ Dead, ☐ Quite sick, ☐ Institutionalized, ☐ Irrelevant

Father's Name _____

☐ Living, ☐ Dead, ☐ Quite sick, ☐ Institutionalized, ☐ Irrelevant

Older Sibling's Name(s) _____

☐ Living, ☐ Dead, ☐ Quite sick, ☐ Institutionalized, ☐ Irrelevant

Younger Sibling's Name(s) _____

☐ Living, ☐ Dead, ☐ Quite sick, ☐ Institutionalized, ☐ Irrelevant

Other Significant Person's Name _____

☐ Living, ☐ Dead, ☐ Quite sick, ☐ Institutionalized, ☐ Irrelevant

Character's General Health: _____

College: _____ Military Service: _____

Early Jobs: _____

Current Job: _____

Desired Job: _____

Hobbies/Interests: _____

Likes/Dislikes: _____

Major Strengths: _____

Major Weaknesses: _____

FATAL FLAW: _____

CHARACTER BIO #3

Full Name _____ Nickname _____

Born in: _____

Resides at/in: _____

Sex _____ Age _____ Race _____ Religion _____

Marital Status_____ Spouse's Name _____

Previous Marriages _____ Name(s)_____

Child One: _____ Sex: _____ Age: _____

Child Two: _____ Sex: _____ Age: _____

Additional Children: _____

Mother's Name _____

☐ Living, ☐ Dead, ☐ Quite sick, ☐ Institutionalized, ☐ Irrelevant

Father's Name _____

☐ Living, ☐ Dead, ☐ Quite sick, ☐ Institutionalized, ☐ Irrelevant

Older Sibling's Name(s) _____

☐ Living, ☐ Dead, ☐ Quite sick, ☐ Institutionalized, ☐ Irrelevant

Younger Sibling's Name(s) _____

☐ Living, ☐ Dead, ☐ Quite sick, ☐ Institutionalized, ☐ Irrelevant

Other Significant Person's Name _____

☐ Living, ☐ Dead, ☐ Quite sick, ☐ Institutionalized, ☐ Irrelevant

Character's General Health: _____

College: _____ Military Service: _____

Early Jobs: _____

Current Job: _____

Desired Job: _____

Hobbies/Interests: _____

Likes/Dislikes: _____

Major Strengths: _____

Major Weaknesses: _____

FATAL FLAW: _____

CHARACTER BIO #4

Full Name _____ Nickname _____

Born in: _____

Resides at/in: _____

Sex _____ Age _____ Race _____ Religion _____

Marital Status _____ Spouse's Name _____

Previous Marriages _____ Name(s) _____

Child One: _____ Sex: _____ Age: _____

Child Two: _____ Sex: _____ Age: _____

Additional Children: _____

Mother's Name _____

☐ Living, ☐ Dead, ☐ Quite sick, ☐ Institutionalized, ☐ Irrelevant

Father's Name _____

☐ Living, ☐ Dead, ☐ Quite sick, ☐ Institutionalized, ☐ Irrelevant

Older Sibling's Name(s) _____

☐ Living, ☐ Dead, ☐ Quite sick, ☐ Institutionalized, ☐ Irrelevant

Younger Sibling's Name(s) _____

☐ Living, ☐ Dead, ☐ Quite sick, ☐ Institutionalized, ☐ Irrelevant

Other Significant Person's Name _____

☐ Living, ☐ Dead, ☐ Quite sick, ☐ Institutionalized, ☐ Irrelevant

Character's General Health: _____

College: _____ Military Service: _____

Early Jobs: _____

Current Job: _____

Desired Job: _____

Hobbies/Interests: _____

Likes/Dislikes: _____

Major Strengths: _____

Major Weaknesses: _____

FATAL FLAW: _____

CHARACTER BIO #5

Full Name _____ Nickname _____
Born in: _____
Resides at/in: _____
Sex _____ Age _____ Race _____ Religion _____
Marital Status _____ Spouse's Name _____
Previous Marriages _____ Name(s) _____
Child One: _____ Sex: _____ Age: _____
Child Two: _____ Sex: _____ Age: _____
Additional Children: _____
Mother's Name _____
☐ Living, ☐ Dead, ☐ Quite sick, ☐ Institutionalized, ☐ Irrelevant
Father's Name _____
☐ Living, ☐ Dead, ☐ Quite sick, ☐ Institutionalized, ☐ Irrelevant
Older Sibling's Name(s) _____
☐ Living, ☐ Dead, ☐ Quite sick, ☐ Institutionalized, ☐ Irrelevant
Younger Sibling's Name(s) _____
☐ Living, ☐ Dead, ☐ Quite sick, ☐ Institutionalized, ☐ Irrelevant
Other Significant Person's Name _____
☐ Living, ☐ Dead, ☐ Quite sick, ☐ Institutionalized, ☐ Irrelevant
Character's General Health: _____
College: _____ Military Service: _____
Early Jobs: _____
Current Job: _____
Desired Job: _____
Hobbies/Interests: _____
Likes/Dislikes: _____
Major Strengths: _____
Major Weaknesses: _____
FATAL FLAW: _____

CHARACTER BIO #6

Full Name _____ **Nickname** _____

Born in: _____

Resides at/in: _____

Sex _____ **Age** _____ **Race** _____ **Religion** _____

Marital Status _____ **Spouse's Name** _____

Previous Marriages _____ **Name(s)** _____

Child One: _____ **Sex:** _____ **Age:** _____

Child Two: _____ **Sex:** _____ **Age:** _____

Additional Children: _____

Mother's Name _____

☐ *Living*, ☐ *Dead*, ☐ *Quite sick*, ☐ *Institutionalized*, ☐ *Irrelevant*

Father's Name _____

☐ *Living*, ☐ *Dead*, ☐ *Quite sick*, ☐ *Institutionalized*, ☐ *Irrelevant*

Older Sibling's Name(s) _____

☐ *Living*, ☐ *Dead*, ☐ *Quite sick*, ☐ *Institutionalized*, ☐ *Irrelevant*

Younger Sibling's Name(s) _____

☐ *Living*, ☐ *Dead*, ☐ *Quite sick*, ☐ *Institutionalized*, ☐ *Irrelevant*

Other Significant Person's Name _____

☐ *Living*, ☐ *Dead*, ☐ *Quite sick*, ☐ *Institutionalized*, ☐ *Irrelevant*

Character's General Health: _____

College: _____ **Military Service:** _____

Early Jobs: _____

Current Job: _____

Desired Job: _____

Hobbies/Interests: _____

Likes/Dislikes: _____

Major Strengths: _____

Major Weaknesses: _____

FATAL FLAW: _____

31

CHARACTER BIO #7

Full Name _____ Nickname _____

Born in: _____

Resides at/in: _____

Sex _____ Age _____ Race _____ Religion _____

Marital Status _____ Spouse's Name _____

Previous Marriages _____ Name(s) _____

Child One: _____ Sex: _____ Age: _____

Child Two: _____ Sex: _____ Age: _____

Additional Children: _____

Mother's Name _____

☐ Living, ☐ Dead, ☐ Quite sick, ☐ Institutionalized, ☐ Irrelevant

Father's Name _____

☐ Living, ☐ Dead, ☐ Quite sick, ☐ Institutionalized, ☐ Irrelevant

Older Sibling's Name(s) _____

☐ Living, ☐ Dead, ☐ Quite sick, ☐ Institutionalized, ☐ Irrelevant

Younger Sibling's Name(s) _____

☐ Living, ☐ Dead, ☐ Quite sick, ☐ Institutionalized, ☐ Irrelevant

Other Significant Person's Name _____

☐ Living, ☐ Dead, ☐ Quite sick, ☐ Institutionalized, ☐ Irrelevant

Character's General Health: _____

College: _____ Military Service: _____

Early Jobs: _____

Current Job: _____

Desired Job: _____

Hobbies/Interests: _____

Likes/Dislikes: _____

Major Strengths: _____

Major Weaknesses: _____

FATAL FLAW: _____

CHARACTER BIO #8

Full Name _____ Nickname _____

Born in: _____

Resides at/in: _____

Sex _____ Age _____ Race _____ Religion _____

Marital Status _____ Spouse's Name _____

Previous Marriages _____ Name(s) _____

Child One: _____ Sex: _____ Age: _____

Child Two: _____ Sex: _____ Age: _____

Additional Children: _____

Mother's Name _____

☐ Living, ☐ Dead, ☐ Quite sick, ☐ Institutionalized, ☐ Irrelevant

Father's Name _____

☐ Living, ☐ Dead, ☐ Quite sick, ☐ Institutionalized, ☐ Irrelevant

Older Sibling's Name(s) _____

☐ Living, ☐ Dead, ☐ Quite sick, ☐ Institutionalized, ☐ Irrelevant

Younger Sibling's Name(s) _____

☐ Living, ☐ Dead, ☐ Quite sick, ☐ Institutionalized, ☐ Irrelevant

Other Significant Person's Name _____

☐ Living, ☐ Dead, ☐ Quite sick, ☐ Institutionalized, ☐ Irrelevant

Character's General Health: _____

College: _____ Military Service: _____

Early Jobs: _____

Current Job: _____

Desired Job: _____

Hobbies/Interests: _____

Likes/Dislikes: _____

Major Strengths: _____

Major Weaknesses: _____

FATAL FLAW: _____

CHARACTER BIO #9

Full Name _____ Nickname _____

Born in: _____

Resides at/in: _____

Sex _____ Age _____ Race _____ Religion _____

Marital Status_____ Spouse's Name _____

Previous Marriages _____ Name(s)_____

Child One: _____ Sex: _____ Age: _____

Child Two: _____ Sex: _____ Age: _____

Additional Children: _____

Mother's Name _____

☐ Living, ☐ Dead, ☐ Quite sick, ☐ Institutionalized, ☐ Irrelevant

Father's Name _____

☐ Living, ☐ Dead, ☐ Quite sick, ☐ Institutionalized, ☐ Irrelevant

Older Sibling's Name(s) _____

☐ Living, ☐ Dead, ☐ Quite sick, ☐ Institutionalized, ☐ Irrelevant

Younger Sibling's Name(s) _____

☐ Living, ☐ Dead, ☐ Quite sick, ☐ Institutionalized, ☐ Irrelevant

Other Significant Person's Name _____

☐ Living, ☐ Dead, ☐ Quite sick, ☐ Institutionalized, ☐ Irrelevant

Character's General Health: _____

College: _____ Military Service: _____

Early Jobs: _____

Current Job: _____

Desired Job: _____

Hobbies/Interests: _____

Likes/Dislikes: _____

Major Strengths: _____

Major Weaknesses: _____

FATAL FLAW: _____

CHARACTER BIO #10

Full Name _____ Nickname _____

Born in: _____

Resides at/in: _____

Sex _____ Age _____ Race _____ Religion _____

Marital Status _____ Spouse's Name _____

Previous Marriages _____ Name(s) _____

Child One: _____ Sex: _____ Age: _____

Child Two: _____ Sex: _____ Age: _____

Additional Children: _____

Mother's Name _____

☐ Living, ☐ Dead, ☐ Quite sick, ☐ Institutionalized, ☐ Irrelevant

Father's Name _____

☐ Living, ☐ Dead, ☐ Quite sick, ☐ Institutionalized, ☐ Irrelevant

Older Sibling's Name(s) _____

☐ Living, ☐ Dead, ☐ Quite sick, ☐ Institutionalized, ☐ Irrelevant

Younger Sibling's Name(s) _____

☐ Living, ☐ Dead, ☐ Quite sick, ☐ Institutionalized, ☐ Irrelevant

Other Significant Person's Name _____

☐ Living, ☐ Dead, ☐ Quite sick, ☐ Institutionalized, ☐ Irrelevant

Character's General Health: _____

College: _____ Military Service: _____

Early Jobs: _____

Current Job: _____

Desired Job: _____

Hobbies/Interests: _____

Likes/Dislikes: _____

Major Strengths: _____

Major Weaknesses: _____

FATAL FLAW: _____

A BRAINSTORMING CHECKLIST

EARTH, WIND, FIRE ,WATER: THE BASICS
SPACE: THE FINAL FRONTIER

The following lists offer a "mix and match" approach to concepting.
The lists are by no means complete, but will serve as a solid starting point.

ENVIRONMENTS
- ☐ **Big Cities/Middle Class**
- ☐ **Big Cities/Upper Class**
- ☐ **Big Cities/Poverty**
- ☐ **Medium Cities/Any of the Above**
- ☐ **Small Towns/Ditto**
- ☐ **Rural Areas/Farms**
- ☐ **Islands**
- ☐ **Foreign Countries**
- ☐ **Inland Cities/Towns/Farms**
- ☐ **Coastal Cities/Towns/Farms**
- ☐ **Businesses**
- ☐ **Schools/Colleges/Universities**
- ☐ **Prisons**

CLIMATES
- ☐ *Cold/Snow*
- ☐ *Total Tundra*
- ☐ *Hot/Humid*
- ☐ *Arid*
- ☐ *Tropical*
- ☐ *Perfect*

TOPOGRAPHY
- ☐ *Flat/Plains*
- ☐ *"Beachy"*
- ☐ *Mountainous*
- ☐ *Desert*
- ☐ *Forest*
- ☐ *Tropical*
- ☐ *Rough/Rocky*
- ☐ *Subterranean/Caves*

NATURAL DISASTERS
- ☐ *Tornadoes*

- ☐ *Hurricanes*
- ☐ *Asteroids*
- ☐ *Earthquakes*
- ☐ *Fires*
- ☐ *Floods*
- ☐ *Blizzards*
- ☐ *Tidal Waves*

HUMAN DISASTERS/CHALLENGES/CHANGES

- ☐ *Death*
- ☐ *Divorce*
- ☐ *Abortion*
- ☐ *Failing Friendship*
- ☐ *Runaway Child*
- ☐ *Serious Illness*
- ☐ *Sudden Disability*
- ☐ *Ship Wreck (Has this been done?)*
- ☐ *Airline/Airplane/Space Vehicle Crash*
- ☐ *Car/Truck Crash*
- ☐ *Explosion*

HUMAN THREATS

- [ ] **Kidnappers**
- [ ] **Burglars**
- [ ] **Economic Recession/Depression**
- [ ] **The IRS**
- [ ] **Landlords**
- [ ] **Collection Agencies**
- [ ] **Angry Ex-Spouses**
- [ ] **Angry Spouses**
- [ ] **Angry Ex-Spouse's Lover/New Spouse**
- [ ] **Angry Spouse's Lover**
- [ ] **Pedophiles**
- [ ] **Rapists**
- [ ] **Hijackers**
- [ ] **Terrorists**
- [ ] **Serial Killers**
- [ ] **Muggers**
- [ ] **Organized Crime**
- [ ] **"Strangers"**
- [ ] **Aliens**

ANIMAL THREATS
- ☐ Wild Animals
- ☐ Domestic Animals
- ☐ Snakes
- ☐ Insects
- ☐ Birds
- ☐ Fish/Whales/Sharks, etc.
- ☐ Zoo Animals
- ☐ Deranged Animals
- ☐ Mythical Beasts/Monsters
- ☐ Alien Beasts

HEALTH & WELL-BEING THREATS
- ☐ Cancer
- ☐ Leukemia
- ☐ AIDS/HIV/STDs.
- ☐ Hepatitis
- ☐ Heart Attack
- ☐ Stroke
- ☐ Psychological Threats

- [ ] *Learning Disabilities*
- [ ] *Attention Deficit Disorder*
- [ ] *Old Age*
- [ ] *An Unknown Virus*
- [ ] *Blindness (aka Vision Impairment)*
- [ ] *Deafness (aka Hearing Impairment)*
- [ ] *Problems Only Viagra Can Cure*

ERA/TIME FRAME

- [ ] *Present Day*
- [ ] *The Future*
- [ ] *Cowboy Days*
- [ ] *Bible Times*
- [ ] *Turn-of-the-Century*
- [ ] *World War I*
- [ ] *World War II*
- [ ] *Korea*
- [ ] *Vietnam*
- [ ] *The Gulf War*
- [ ] *The Next War(s)*

- ☐ *The 40s*
- ☐ *The 50s*
- ☐ *The 60s*
- ☐ *The 70s*
- ☐ *The 80s*
- ☐ *The 90s*

THEMES

- ☐ *Survival*
- ☐ *Daring Rescues*
- ☐ *Buddies*
- ☐ *Friend-Against-Friend*
- ☐ *Good Versus Evil*
- ☐ *Animal/Human "Teams"*
- ☐ *Unfamiliar Surroundings (Fish Out of Water)*
- ☐ *Coming-of-Age*
- ☐ *Personal Growth*
- ☐ *Success in Competition*
- ☐ *Paranormal Events/People*

LIFE'S COMMON EVENTS

(Most of these things take place in most peoples' lives: some are inevitable. The order, of course, varies among individuals.)

- ☐ **Birth**
- ☐ **Childhood**
- ☐ **Birthdays**
- ☐ **Siblings**
- ☐ **Growth**
- ☐ **School**
- ☐ **Friendships**
- ☐ **Injuries**
- ☐ **Illnesses**
- ☐ **Adolescence**
- ☐ **Sports**
- ☐ **Clubs/Affiliations**
- ☐ **Falling in Love**
- ☐ **Career**
- ☐ **Courtship**
- ☐ **Marriage**
- ☐ **Anniversaries**

- ☐ Sex
- ☐ Pregnancy
- ☐ Giving Birth
- ☐ Parenthood
- ☐ Home Ownership
- ☐ Moving/Relocating
- ☐ Career Change
- ☐ Accidents
- ☐ Burglaries/Thefts
- ☐ Parenting Teenagers
- ☐ Divorce
- ☐ Remarriage
- ☐ Blending of Families
- ☐ Death of Parents
- ☐ Death of In-laws
- ☐ Death of Siblings
- ☐ Grown Children Living at Home
- ☐ Marriages of Children
- ☐ Middle-age Crisis
- ☐ Becoming Grandparents

- ☐ *Failing Health*
- ☐ *Old Age*
- ☐ *Living with Grown Children*
- ☐ *Death of a Spouse or Child*
- ☐ *Nursing Home*
- ☐ *Coma/Complete Incapacitation*
- ☐ *Death*

LIFE'S MORE UNUSUAL EVENTS:
(These things happen to some people, but are less common.)

- ☐ *Accidental Death*
- ☐ *Adoption*
- ☐ *Military Service*
- ☐ *Dying in Battle*
- ☐ *Death or Life-threatening Illness of a Young Child*
- ☐ *A Big Lottery/Gambling Win*
- ☐ *Incredible Success in Business or Career*
- ☐ *House Fire*

- ☐ *Huge Inheritance*
- ☐ *Getting Fired*
- ☐ *Multiple Divorces/Remarriages*
- ☐ *Prison Term*
- ☐ *Drug Problem*
- ☐ *Miraculous (Faith) Healing*
- ☐ *Suicide (Self, Spouse, Child or Friend)*
- ☐ *Space Travel*
- ☐ *Box Office Refund for a Lousy Movie*
- ☐ *Courtside Seats at a Lakers Playoff Game*
- ☐ *Murder of Self/Spouse/Child/Friend*
- ☐ *Rape*
- ☐ *Election to High Political Office*
- ☐ *A Return Phone Call From An Agent*
- ☐ *Sale of a "Spec" Screenplay*

LIFE'S PLANES:
- ☐ *Physical*
- ☐ *Mental*
- ☐ *Emotional*
- ☐ *Behavioral*
- ☐ *Sexual*
- ☐ *Intellectual*
- ☐ *Spiritual*
- ☐ *Supernatural*

DEATH'S PLANES:
- ☐ *Heaven*
- ☐ *Hell*
- ☐ *Nowhere in Particular*
- ☐ *Somewhere Else (?)*

Now, wasn't that fun? Bet you came up with at least five hot ideas! And to think, just yesterday you had a "normal" job.

ABSOLUTE, FOR SURE, 100% EFFECTIVE WAYS TO BREAK UP WRITER'S BLOCK AND RELEASE YOUR CREATIVE BILES:

☐ *Go to an art gallery. Stare at a painting and ask, "What story is this trying to tell?"* Some don't tell any story, but that's not your problem. It's the artist's.

☐ *Shoot candid video of complete strangers and add some of their mannerisms to your characters.*

☐ *Listen to a radio station that plays the kind of music you don't normally listen to. (Country, Rap, Rock, Classical)*

☐ *Listen to a talk radio personality you can't stand.* As far as I'm concerned, that would be ALL of them.

☐ *New computers always have better ideas. Buy one and blow up the old one or give it to charity—unless it's over six months old, in which case no charity would actually want it. (Remember to save your script on a disk or something.)*

☐ *Go clean up a two-mile stretch of highway. The stuff you find will trigger a bunch of stories.*

☐ *Visit someone in a retirement center or nursing home.*

☐ *Watch a soap on TV. Your worst stuff will look brilliant by comparison.*

Unless, of course, you write for the soaps in which case this was a terrible insult and I apologize profusely. Really. I do.

☐ *Read a book by F. Scott Fitzgerald.*

☐ *Take a shower.*

☐ *Paint or wallpaper something.*

☐ *Read a children's book.*

☐ *Go to the library.*

☐ *Go to a movie.*

☐ *Two words: "MAD Magazine."*

☐ *Begin work on another project— something you wouldn't normally write. (A cartoon, a book, a stage play.)*

☐ *Rent a foreign film—no subtitles. (Don't cheat by knowing the language.)*

FUTURE SCREENWRITER'S CHECKLIST:

- ☐ *Go to lots of movies*
- ☐ *Rent lots of movies*
- ☐ *Watch lots of movies with the sound OFF (To see how scenes are handled)*
- ☐ *Listen to the sound track only (To get the drift of how dialogue works)*
- ☐ *Take notes on everything (a journal)*
- ☐ *Buy 3" X 5" cards in lots of colors*
- ☐ *Buy a portable computer*
- ☐ *Get "FINAL DRAFT" or other bigtime screenwriting program* "Final Draft" for PC or Mac, from Final Draft, Inc.: 1-800-231-4055
- ☐ *Subscribe to "SCENARIO" or read lots of screenplays from other sources*
- ☐ *Subscribe to "THE HOLLYWOOD REPORTER – (Tuesday edition)*
- ☐ *Find a really good agent*
- ☐ *"Date" a successful producer*

CRASH COURSES: When you want to learn a whole bunch of stuff in a short amount of time, call these people.

Hauge: Michael Hauge is the author of WRITING SCREENPLAYS THAT SELL, a must-read book for perspiring screenwriters. He's also a script consultant who offers seminars or a regular basis. Contact him at Hilltop Productions, P.O. Box 55728, Sherman Oaks, CA 91413. The phone number is 1-800-477-1947, fax is 818-986-1504, and e-mail is mhauge@juno.com.

McKee: Robert McKee, author of STORY, has numerous Oscar® and Emmy® winners among his former students. His three-day classes are offered throughout the year in New York and Los Angeles. Call Toll-Free: 1-888-67-MCKEE (676-3924), fax 310-318-3924, or go to his Web site at www.mckeestory.com for more information.

Seger: Linda Seger is prominent in WOMEN IN FILM and has written a number of books on the screenwriting process, including MAKING A GOOD SCRIPT GREAT, CREATING UNFORGETTABLE CHARACTERS, and WHEN WOMEN CALL THE SHOTS. A "script doctor" who also offers seminars, Dr. Seger can be reached at 310-390-1951, or (fax) 310-398-7541.

Gavigan: Bart Gavigan, who lives and works in the U.K., frequently comes to the U.S. to teach seminars. We will try to post his U.S. schedule on our Web site: www.prioritymm.com. In the mean time, his audio cassette series, THE SCREENWRITER'S STORY STRUCTURE WORKSHOP, is available from Priority Multimedia Group, Inc. Order through the Web (www.prioritymm.com), order by phone at 1-800-5-GOTTRY (1-800-546-8879), order by fax (602-831-7373), or use the order form at the back of this book.

Oh, yeah. Be sure to read all these books:

- ☐ **Story**

  Robert McKee *(ISBN: 0-06-039168-5)*

- ☐ **Making A Good Script Great**

  Linda Seger *(ISBN: 0-573-69921-6)*

- ☐ **Creating Unforgettable Characters**

  Linda Seger *(ISBN: 0-8050-1171-4)*

- ☐ **Lew Hunter's Screenwriting 434**

  Lew Hunter *(ISBN: 0-399-51838-X)*

- ☐ **Screenplay**

  Syd Field *(ISBN: 0-452-26347-8)*

- ☐ **The Screenwriter's Workbook**

  Syd Field *(ISBN: 0-440-58225-3)*

- ☐ **Selling a Screenplay**

  Syd Field *(ISBN: 0-440-50244-6)*

- ☐ **The Screenwriter's Bible**

  David Trottier *(ISBN: 1-879505-26-6)*

Tired of reading yet? But wait!

There's more!

- [ ] **Writing Screenplays That Sell**
  Michael Hauge *(ISBN: 0-06-272500-9)*

- [ ] **Writing Treatments That Sell**
  Kenneth Atchity and Chi-Li Wong
  (ISBN:)-8050-4283-0)

- [ ] **Opening The Doors To Hollywood**
  Carlos De Abreu/Howard Jay Smith
  (ISBN: 1-884025-04-8)

- [ ] **How to Sell Your Screenplay**
  Carl Sautter *(ISBN: 0-942257-24-3)*

- [ ] **How to Enter Screenplay Contests & Win**
  Erik Joseph *(ISBN: 0-943728-88-6)*

- [ ] **Filmmaker's Dictionary**
  Ralph S. Singleton *(ISBN: 0-943728-08-8)*

All of these wonderful books are available from your favorite bookseller. Just ask for them by ISBN! And, if you read Lew Hunter's SCREENWRITING 434 (highly recommended), you'll probably rush right back to the store to buy POETICS by Aristotle (various publishers) and THE ART OF DRAMATIC WRITING, by Lajos Egri (ISBN: 0-671-21332-6). Unless you have a photographic memory, you'll want to have a dictionary and thesaurus handy, too.

Have I read all these books? Well, I'm on page 1109 of "Webster's."

You might also want to buy a copy of:
- ☐ **Hollywood Creative Directory**
  Call (310) 315-4815

There are some worthwhile sites on the Internet, too:
- ☐ **www.inhollywood.com**
  (There is a fee for some services.)
- ☐ **www.screenwriters.com**
  (Enter www.screenwriters.com/Hauge/index.html to get directly to Michael Hauge's page.)
- ☐ **www.hollywoodreporter.com**
  (There is a fee for some services.)
- ☐ **www.hollywoodnetwork.com**
- ☐ **www.wga.org**
  (Some information is restricted to Writers Guild Members.)
- ☐ **www.scripts-onscreen.com**
  (There is a charge for posting your listing.)
- ☐ **http://lcweb.loc.gov/copyright/**
  (You can download and print copyright forms from this site.)

And, of course, MY favorite Web Site:
- ☐ **www.6FU.com** *(NO FEES or other access charges!)*

All finished writing your first draft? Here are your next steps:

- ☐ *Proofreed the script carfully.*
- ☐ *Register it with Writers Guild of America west (WGAw).*

  (Send one unbound copy along with $20 (the non-member's registration fee) to Writers Guild of America west, 7000 West Third Street, Los Angeles, CA 90048. Include your name, address, phone number and Social Security number on the cover page.)

- ☐ *Register a copy with the U.S. Copyright Office. (Obtain forms off the World Wide Web.)*
- ☐ *Ask five friends who will give you honest feedback to read your script.*
- ☐ *Sell it to a Famous Hollywood Producer for $500,000 or so.*
- ☐ *Begin work on your next script. After all, this IS going to be your career, right?*

NOTES:

THE SCREENWRITER'S STORY STRUCTURE WORKSHOP

Bart Gavigan

SO YOU WANNA BE A SCREENWRITER?

Well, don't we all?

Here's help! This is the best "how to" I've found yet.

Now, I have to admit that there are some great books on screenwriting out there. (Michael Hauge's WRITING SCREENPLAYS THAT SELL comes to mind. As do MAKING A GOOD SCRIPT GREAT by Linda Seger and LEW HUNTER'S SCREENWRITING 434 by Lew Hunter.)

And I have to confess that I've always wanted to take in Robert McKee's story structure classes in LA or NY. But I don't live in LA or NY, so attending the class would involve a good-size commitment of both time and money.

Enter Bart Gavigan's 13-cassette audio class, THE SCREENWRITER'S STORY STRUCTURE WORKSHOP! I can take these cassettes everywhere and anywhere and learn at my own pace. I've listened to them four times in my car, and every time I've gone back home and re-written my current "script-in-process." And I believe every time it gets better. Bart has written just about everything—short-form stuff for the BBC to feature films—and his step-by-step learning program will lead you through Inspiration, Characters, Conflict, Foreshadowing, Mood, Tempo, Pace, Turning the Film, Sub-Plot, Endings, Genre, and a whole bunch of other good stuff.

You might think the price—$179.95—is a bit stiff. But we're so sure you'll get your money's worth that we're offering it with a full 30-day money back guarantee. If you're not completely satisfied, just return the tapes in salable condition for a full refund. (We trust you not to copy them—people who do that kind of thing usually end up penniless in some Hollywood gutter. Deservedly so.) So give your "good" script the chance to be "great." Order THE SCREENWRITER'S STORY STRUCTURE WORKSHOP today!

-- Steve Gottry, Perspiring Screenwriter

Produced by Tim Mahoney for Mahoney Broadcast Media Group, © 1995.

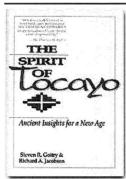

THE SPIRIT OF TOCAYO was written for people who:

- Enjoy a good story for its own sake.
- Believe that anything is possible.
- Ask more questions than most of their friends.
- Are on a quest for wisdom.
- Can imagine a better world.
- Aren't afraid to answer the call of the heart.

If you've read and enjoyed books such as THE CELESTINE PROPHECY, this book is for you! If you're questioning what kind of difference spirituality can make in someone's life, this book could point you toward some answers! Available at bookstores or direct from Priority.

THE REVIEWS TELL THE STORY.

ZIG ZIGLAR (Motivational speaker and best-selling author): "A reality-based, optimistically-sound practical why and how-to guide to business success in the '90s. It's concise, clear cut, easy to read and practical in application because of its sound ethical base. Good stuff!"

DR. DENIS WAITLEY (Author of THE PSYCHOLOGY OF WINNING): "If you plan to own, manage or be part of a profitable growth business, read this book. If you plan to fail, give it to your competitors. It is on target in today's global village."

HON. ROBERT F. BENNETT (United States Senator): "As one who has run a small business, I recognize the genuine article when I see it. Steve Gottry has truly 'been there,' and his writing style will take you there, too. I wish every member of Congress were familiar with the concepts in this book."

OPTIONS is the intensely personal story of a woman's search for love, understanding and forgiveness—and the choices she made that robbed her of the happiness she longed for.

Candidly sharing the pain of loss and her escape from a brutal relationship, Karla Gottry offers hope for the healing of even the deepest of scars. Here is gentle, caring help from someone who has truly been there. And made it through. If you know a woman who is living with the pain of past decisions—or is facing a future of uncertainty—give her this book. If you are that woman yourself, read this book.

But be prepared: This story won't just touch your heart—it will break it.

EQUIP YOURSELF WITH THE TOOLS YOU NEED TO TAKE CHARGE OF YOUR DESTINY AND CLIMB THE LADDER OF SUCCESS!

There are a lot of books out there that relate business theory, but very few that teach basic management growth skills in easy-to-swallow capsules. **CAREER GEAR** begins with topics such as Training, Learning, Communication and Teamwork, and builds to a set of must-use checklists that will fine-tune your management skills in such areas as Effective Leadership and Professional Work Habits. This book will inspire you, motivate you, and improve your performance as a manager!

"A wise and practical book—it will not only help those starting out on a business career, but also anyone who manages people."
-- Joseph C. Miller, Professor of Marketing
Indiana University School of Business

ORDER FORM

If these products are not available from your favorite bookseller, please use this form to order by Fax or Mail – or order through our Web site at: www.prioritymm.com.

Name: _____

Address: _____

City: _____ State: _____ Zip: _____

Phone: _____ Fax: _____ e-mail: _____

PRODUCT	QUANTITY	PRICE EACH	TOTAL
THE SCREENWRITER'S STORY STRUCTURE WORKSHOP Series of tapes by Bart Gavigan – Product code: MAH-1-95	_____	$179.95	_____
THE SCREENWRITER'S STORY PLANNING GUIDE Steven R. Gottry – ISBN 0-9667483-0-1	_____	$7.99	_____
COMMON SENSE BUSINESS IN A NONSENSE ECONOMY By Steven R. Gottry – ISBN 0-89384-259-1	_____	$14.95	_____
THE SPIRIT OF TOCAYO By Steven R. Gottry and Richard A. Jacobsen ISBN 1-886158-01-0	_____	$16.95	_____
CAREER GEAR By Linda Jensvold Bauer – ISBN 1-886158-07-X	_____	$8.95	_____
OPTIONS Karla S. Gottry – ISBN 1-886158-11-8	_____	$4.95	_____
AZ RESIDENTS MUST ADD CURRENT SALES TAX:			$ _____
Shipping (Add $3.00 for first item, $1.00 more for each additional item)			$ _____
TOTAL OF ORDER			$ _____

PAYMENT METHOD: ☐ CHECK OR MONEY ORDER ENCLOSED (Payable to "PRIORITY MULTIMEDIA GROUP, INC.")

☐ VISA ☐ MASTERCARD ☐ AMERICAN EXPRESS

ACCOUNT NUMBER: _____ – _____ – _____ EXPIRES: Month ☐☐ Year ☐☐

SIGNATURE (Required) _____

MAIL TO: **PRIORITY MULTIMEDIA GROUP • BOX 41540 • MESA, AZ 85202-1540**, or: FAX TO: (602) 831-7373.
Phone Orders with Credit Card: 1-800-5-GOTTRY (1-800-546-8879). Allow 2-4 weeks for delivery.